Children of the World

My Life in
JAMAICA

Patience Coster

Cavendish
Square

New York

Published in 2015 by Cavendish Square Publishing, LLC
243 5th Avenue, Suite 136, New York, NY 10016

First Edition

Website: cavendishsq.com

This publication represents the opinions and views of the author based on his or her personal experience, knowledge, and research. The information in this book serves as a general guide only. The author and publisher have used their best efforts in preparing this book and disclaim liability rising directly or indirectly from the use and application of this book.

CPSIA Compliance Information: Batch #WW15CSQ

All websites were available and accurate when this book was sent to press.

Library of Congress Cataloging-in-Publication Data

Coster, Patience.
My life in Jamaica / by Patience Coster.
p. cm. — (Children of the world)
Includes index.
ISBN 978-1-50260-052-3 (hardcover) ISBN 978-1-50260-054-7 (paperback)
ISBN 978-1-50260-053-0 (ebook)
1. Jamaica — Juvenile literature. 2. Jamaica — Social life and customs — Juvenile literature. 3. Children — Jamaica — Juvenile literature. I. Coster, Patience. II. Title.
F1868.2 C695 2015
972.92—d23

Editor: Joe Harris
Designer: Ian Winton

All photography courtesy of Andrew P. Smith / Demotix / Corbis

Printed in the United States of America

Contents

My Home	4
Breakfast	6
Time to Go	8
The School Bus	10
My School	12
Lessons Begin	14
Break Time	16
Math Class	18
Lunchtime	20
Afternoon Lessons	22
Dance Class	24
Shopping and Homework	26
Dinner and Bedtime	28
Glossary	30
Further Information	31
Index	32

My Home

Hi! My name is Zola. I live in Liguanea, a town on the outskirts of Kingston, Jamaica. I am ten years old.

There are four people in my family – Dad, Mom, my little sister Tany, and me. I share a bedroom with Tany.

Zola says ...

Our bedroom is crowded. Sometimes it's hard to find stuff!

Oh, that's where they were! I've found all my books for school today.

My Country

Jamaica is a mountainous island in the Caribbean Sea. Around three million people live here. One-third of all Jamaicans live in the capital city, Kingston.

Breakfast

Before breakfast, I wash and get dressed. Like most children in Jamaica, I wear a uniform to school.

My uniform is a brown skirt and tie with the school **emblem**, and a white short-sleeved shirt.

6

Dad fries pancakes for breakfast. On other days we might have boiled bananas, potatoes, or **yams**. While breakfast is cooking, Dad gets my packed lunch together.

Zola says ...

I always give thanks for my food before eating.

Starting the Day

In Jamaica most people eat cooked breakfasts. Some people have fried or boiled eggs with **cornmeal** or banana porridge.

Time to Go

Mom works until late at a factory, so Dad is in charge of getting us to school in the mornings.

I play a quick game with Tany on my mobile phone. She will be starting school next term.

Dad gives me money for the bus and to buy a snack.

Zola says ...

Good manners are an important part of family life. I always try to remember to say please and thank you!

Mom makes sure my hair is tidy before I leave.

Money and Schooling

The Jamaican government wants every child to be in school. However, some families can't **afford** the bus fare to send their children to school.

The School Bus

Dad walks with me to the bus stop. It is just a short walk from my house and the journey to school only takes five minutes.

The school day starts at eight o'clock. Dad is worried that we won't make it to the bus stop on time!

The bus takes students to the primary and senior schools – it can get quite crowded and hot!

Zola says ...

I told you we would make it on time, Dad!

Climate

Jamaica is close to the equator. It has a tropical climate, which means it is hot and **humid** all year round. It is sometimes hit by **hurricanes** in the summer months.

My School

The name of my school is St. Francis Primary and Infant School. Around nine hundred children attend the school. There are forty-eight students in my class.

I wait with my friend Leon for the teacher to arrive.

12

Each day we have different **responsibilities**. We might be in charge of class **devotion** or collecting the books at the end of a lesson.

Zola says ...

For devotion, we take turns reading a passage from the Bible out loud.

Religion in Jamaica

St. Francis is a **Roman Catholic** school. It was founded by Catholic nuns in 1890. Nowadays, 62 percent of people in Jamaica are **Protestants**.

8.40 AM

Lessons Begin

We take our seats for the first lesson of the day, which is science. Today we are learning about air **pollution**.

Jamaica is a famously beautiful country. Tourists travel here from all over the world. However, like many countries, we have problems with pollution.

Zola says ...
We all have a lot to say about this subject!

The teacher asks us to think about how we can stop pollution. We split into small study groups.

Primary Education

In Jamaica we attend primary school for six years, between the ages of six and eleven. All our lessons are taught in English.

Break Time

At break time, we all go out to the yard to chat and play. It's a hot day, so we stay in the shade.

Dad has packed an orange for my snack. It has been grown right here in Jamaica, and it's delicious!

Zola says ...

Mary is my best friend. We are always laughing when we are together.

My friend Lisa hasn't brought a drink, so I share my juice with her. On a day like today, even standing around talking can be thirsty work!

Jamaican Farms

Jamaican crops such as sugar, rum, coffee, bananas, and yams are shipped all over the world. Jamaica's farms are very important, because they bring money into the country.

10:15 AM

After break, we have math. I like adding and subtracting, but find some things, like multiplying decimals, quite hard.

2.5 × 1.5 = 3.75

Multiplying Decimals

Multiplying decimals can be done in the same way as ordinary multiplication but be sure that the product has the total number of decimal places contained in the problem.

Problem: Multiply 3.4 by .2
This problem has 2 decimal places
therefore

2.46
× 0.3
8

I get a bit stuck when I have to work out sums in front of the class.

CHALK

1.25 × 2.5 = 3.125

Our teacher, Mrs. Blake-Palmer, gets us to sing a song about math to make us more confident.

Zola says ...

We sing the song to the tune of Bob Marley's "Three Little Birds."

Jamaican Music

Jamaican musician Bob Marley was famous for a type of music called reggae. Reggae has been around since 1960. It's a kind of dance music with a bouncy beat. Other types of music that started out in Jamaica include ska and dancehall.

Lunchtime

12:00 PM

Around noon I eat my packed lunch in the classroom. Today I have a beef **patty**. Then I hang out with my friends Mary and Rashona in the yard.

We play handclapping games like "Four White Horses" and "Lemonade Crunchy Ice."

Zola says ...
We sing or chant a song as we clap in rhythm — it's good fun!

When lunchtime is over, we line up and say a prayer before going back into class. We have to be really still and quiet!

Playground Games

If someone remembers to bring a rope or two, we play **double-dutch skipping** and sometimes **handball**. S-T-O-P is another handclap game we play, which is a version of dodge or tag.

Afternoon Lessons

After lunch we are all back in class to practice our reading. Then we have lessons in language arts and music.

In language arts we are learning how to talk and write about friendship.

In music we are listening to examples and learning how to recognize written notes and symbols.

The school day ends at 2:30PM. We are all dismissed and I go to catch the bus home.

Zola says...
I'm glad it's not far to the bus stop — my school books are heavy!

Languages

Jamaica is an English-speaking country. We also speak Jamaican patois (PA-twa), which mixes together words from English and African languages.

Dance Class

On Monday evenings I go to a dance class at a nearby church. When I get home I have some **crackers** and cheese. Then I change into my dance clothes.

We are practicing for a performance at this Sunday's church service.

We do warm-up exercises first.

Last month our group won a gold medal at the national schools' dance competition.

Folk Dances

There are many traditional Jamaican folk dances. Some, such as the maypole dance, originated in Europe. Others, such as jonkunnu (JON-ka-new), dinki-mini, and maroon, originated in Africa.

Shopping and Homework

Dad brings Tany along to pick me up from dance class. We go to a supermarket to buy some groceries.

We need to get a drink for my packed lunch tomorrow.

On the weekend we usually go to the local market to buy fruit and vegetables.

Before dinner I do my math homework.

Zola says ...

I'm going to keep practicing my decimals until I get them right!

Market

Jamaican markets sell different local crafts ranging from **batik** (ba-TEEK) fabrics and baskets to wood carvings. Dolphin and fish carvings are made from the Jamaican national tree, *lignum vitae (LIG-num VY-tee)*, or tree of life.

Dinner and Bedtime

I eat dinner with Tany. Dad waits for Mom to come home so that they can eat together.

Zola says ...

We have steamed fish with yams and **callaloo**.

We may watch TV after dinner or play a card game like "Donkey" or "Go Fish."

Before bed, Tany and I wash our faces, brush our teeth, and say our prayers.

Food in Jamaica

Jamaican cooking is spicy and tasty. People from many different countries have settled here in the past four hundred years. They have all made their mark on the local food! The national dish is **ackee** and **salt-fish**.

Glossary

ackee The national fruit of Jamaica – it looks a bit like a lychee.

afford To have enough money to pay for something.

batik A method of using wax on fabrics to create patterns. The waxed areas of the fabric resist the dye, while the unwaxed areas take the dye.

callaloo A Jamaican dish made with a type of spinach, salt, and onions.

cornmeal A food made by crushing maize (corn) into a powder.

crackers Thin, crispy baked bread products.

devotion Bible class to start the day in school.

double-dutch skipping A type of skipping where two ropes are used and turned in opposite directions.

emblem A badge or symbol.

handball A game in which a ball is hit against a wall with the hand.

humid Hot, clammy, and damp.

hurricane A storm with a very strong wind that usually causes lots of damage.

patty A small mass of minced food, usually meat.

pollution Allowing something harmful to living things to escape into the air, water, or soil.

Protestant A member of the Christian Church that is separate from the Roman Catholic Church.

responsibilities Things that you have to do.

Roman Catholic A Christian Church of which the Pope is the supreme head.

salt-fish A type of fish, usually cod, that has been preserved in salt.

yam The long, thick root of a tropical plant that is eaten as a starchy vegetable, much like a potato or sweet potato.

Further Information

Websites

http://jamaicans.com/childsguide
  Learn about Jamaican culture, recipes, stories, and more.

http://kids.nationalgeographic.com/explore/countries/jamaica.html
  This website has facts about Jamaican geography, nature, people and culture, government, economy, and history.

www.activityvillage.co.uk/jamaica
  Have fun learning about Jamaica with games and puzzles.

www.everyculture.com/Ja-Ma/Jamaica.html
  This website covers the history, food, economy, and culture of Jamaica.

www.sciencekids.co.nz/sciencefacts/countries/jamaica.html
  Find out facts and figures about Jamaica.

Further Reading

Brownlie, Alison. *Letters from Around the World: Jamaica*. London, England: Cherrytree Books, 2009.

Calway, Gareth. *Read On: Bound for Jamaica*. Glasgow, Scotland: Collins Educational, 2012.

Capek, Michael. *Country Explorers: Jamaica*. Minneapolis, MN: Lerner Publications, 2010.

Savage, Jeff. *Amazing Athletes: Usain Bolt*. Minneapolis, MN: Lerner Publications, 2012.

Williams, Colleen. *Carribbean Today: Jamaica*. Broomall, PA: Mason Crest Publishers, 2009.

Zephaniah, Benjamin. *World Alphabet: Jamaica*. London, England: Frances Lincoln Children's Books, 2009.

Index

ackee 29
air pollution 12–13

bananas 7, 17
Bob Marley 19
break time 16–17
breakfast 6–7

callaloo 28
capital city 5
Caribbean Sea 5
class size 12
climate 11
coffee 17
cornmeal 7
crafts 27
crops 17

dancing 24–25
devotion 13
dinner 28

English 15, 23

family 4
farms 17
folk dances 25
food 6–7, 16–17, 20, 24, 26, 28–29

games 8, 20–21, 28

hurricanes 11

Jamaica 4–7, 11, 13–17, 19, 23, 25, 27, 29
Jamaican government 9

Kingston 4–5

language arts 22
lessons 14–15, 18–19, 22–23
Liguanea 4
lunch 20

manners 9
markets 26–27
math 18–19, 27
mobile phone 8
music 19, 23

national dish 29
national tree 27

patois 23
population 5
prayers 7, 29
primary school 11–12, 15
Protestants 13

reggae 19
religion 7, 13, 21
Roman Catholics 13
rum 17

salt-fish 29

school 5–6, 8–13, 15, 23, 25
school age 15
school bus 9, 10–11, 23
school day 10
science 14–15
shopping 26–27
study groups 15
sugar 17
summer 11

television 28
tourists 14

uniform 6

work 8

yams 7, 17, 28